Who's Got The Ring?

NOMI WHALEN

For more information or copies contact:
WHALENBOOKS
912 Larch Place
Canmore, Alberta T1W 1S5

NATIONAL LIBRARY OF CANADA CATALOGUING IN PUBLICATION DATA

Whalen, Nomi, 1932–
    Who's Got The Ring?: Wedding tales by one of Canada's most Popular Marriage Commissioners / by Nomi Whalen; editing and foreword by Madeline Hombert; illustrations by Audrey Mabee.

ISBN 0-9733251-0-0

    1. Whalen, Nomi, 1932– 2. Weddings—Anecdotes. 3. Marriage celebrants—Anecdotes. I. Hombert, Madeline, 1944– II. Title.

HQ745.W43 2003   392.5   C2003-905417-9

Illustrations by Audrey Mabee
Editing by Madeline Hombert
Layout by the Vancouver Desktop Publishing Centre
Printed in China

Welcome to the wonderful memories of NOMI WHALEN, one of Canada's busiest — and arguably most popular — Marriage Commissioners.

At publishing, Nomi had performed over six thousand weddings, and she has no intention of slowing down.

Weddings in planes, weddings on dog sleds, weddings in tattoo parlors. There's not much that Nomi hasn't experienced while guiding couples on their way to wedded bliss.

This book will give you a glimpse at some of her adventures.

FOREWORD

It was at one of those public gatherings over thirty years ago where faces melt into a blur and the numerous introductions are soon forgotten. Nomi Whalen was already a "mover and shaker" in Calgary's art, theatre & political circles and I was a teenage bride struggling with babies and my first home. I was in awe of this woman who seemed to always be DOING IMPORTANT THINGS. She was a teacher, an actress, a civic alderwoman and a psychologist. She never stopped.

In 2000, our paths crossed again. This time we were peers and it was the right place and the right time for us to form a strong bond. I had approached Nomi to become involved in a television and book project I was developing and although that project didn't get off the ground, our friendship did and I became her editor and trusted "sister-friend."

Meeting Audrey Mabee came shortly after and I was in full agreement with Nomi that Audrey's illustrations would be perfect for her book. The drawings are exquisitely whimsical and truly bring Nomi's memories to life.

This book is about weddings, or, as we like to refer to them, NOMI'S WEDDINGS, and it is written by the Commissioner who feels she is the alternate Mother of the Bride at every marriage she solemnizes.

A hundred books couldn't cover half of the ceremonies she's performed. The twenty-five we've selected are just the tip of the iceberg — a microscopic look at love and marriage, and they reflect a wonderful part of Nomi's life.

Nomi has the job she was born to do.

Enjoy.

My wonderful husband, Ed Whalen, was so enthused about this little book and was delighted with the stories, most of which were written before we lost him in 2001.

He loved and supported me in everything I did.

For you, my darling!

TABLE OF CONTENTS

The First Time

"Acne, apathy & chewing gum"

I was a member of Calgary City Council, a brand new marriage commissioner and very proud of my office in the municipal center of such a thriving city. About to perform my very first wedding ceremony in City Hall, I was nervous but looking forward to this important career milestone.

I left my office feeling very official, very proper, very much the picture of a dignified MARRIAGE COMMISSIONER.

And I looked forward to meeting the lucky pair of citizens who had chosen to have their union solemnized at such a proper place by such a proper member of the civic council.

There they were.

Two awkward teenagers, not yet finished with acne. Both casually chewing gum. Neither one overly excited nor impressed. Prepared for a wedding? They didn't even bring witnesses!

Right then I wondered if I had made a huge mistake.
Where were the flowers?
The music?

Where was my fantasy of joining teary-eyed lovers amid rose petals and joyous friends? Where was the damn photographer?

After a moment of inward pouting, I adjusted my new robe and rounded up a couple of clerks to act as witnesses. The non-plussed teens filled out the necessary forms and mumbled "I do" when prompted. When the ceremony was over, the groom handed over the fee, picked up the certificate and they left. No kisses, no smiles.
No NOTHING!
So much for my foray into the wonderful world of weddings.
Nomi's big "first."
Two bored kids. No excitement.
No romance.
I just hope that things got better for them as the years passed.

They had to!

Who's Got The Ring?

"The best behaved ring bearer ever."

At the time they booked their ceremony, the attractive young couple had told me to expect a seven-year-old ringbearer.

The day arrived and when they met me outside the hotel, I noticed a sense of apprehension.

After the initial nervous welcome, the source of their anxiety was revealed.

The seven-year-old was none other than their pet Cocker Spaniel.

They had left out this one small detail fearing that I might refuse to include a canine in the wedding party.

After assuring the bride and groom that there were no legal reasons preventing their precious pet from participating, and that I was more amused than concerned, we went into the reception room. The groom, best man and I took our places and the wedding began.

Once the maid of honor entered and took her place, the groom firmly said "BENTLEY" and all eyes turned to the doorway to see the little dog fully decked out in formal tuxedo and bow tie. Attached to his back was a satin pillow with the wedding rings.

The little star proudly marched down the aisle, presented his important cargo to his master and remained still as the bride entered. He was attentive and quiet throughout the whole ceremony.

The couple needn't have worried about their surprise attendant.

Bentley was arguably the best-behaved ring bearer of my entire career.

Backyard Saturday Night

"A sea of flesh-colored cones bobbing in the breeze"

One Saturday night, I found myself in a backyard amidst sixty very "happy" guests — all of which had obviously taken full advantage of a well-stocked bar. There was a lot of giggling and shuffling around but I was busy checking my notes so didn't really investigate.

When the bride and groom left the house, I arranged them in the usual wedding formation, facing me, their backs to their friends. Just as well. When I looked up and over their shoulders I immediately saw the source of the laughter and suspicious behavior.

Each and every guest had donned a huge CONE HEAD in honor of the couple's favorite "Saturday Night Live" segment. What a sight to behold!

They were all shaking from trying to control their laughter and it took every ounce of self-control I could muster to avoid cracking up as well. I simply focused on the sincere faces of the bride and groom and avoided looking past them at all costs.

Usually, part way through, I ask the bride and groom to turn slightly and face each other to recite their vows. This time? No way! I couldn't take the slightest chance that they may catch sight of the sea of flesh-colored cones bobbing in the breeze.

By some miracle, I completed the ceremony and managed to preserve the dignity of this life-long commitment.

Then, after pronouncing them husband and wife, I signaled them to turn and face their family and friends.

The bride and groom and everyone in the yard erupted in shrieks and gales of laughter.

This couple will always remember their "Conehead" friends and their very special tribute to their personal "Saturday Night" memory.

Manure, Mounts & Marriage

"Fortunately, the mare they chose for me was as old as I was"

When you're a marriage commissioner in ranch country, you have to expect a few western-style weddings, so I wasn't surprised when I was asked to meet the couple and their guests at a barn.

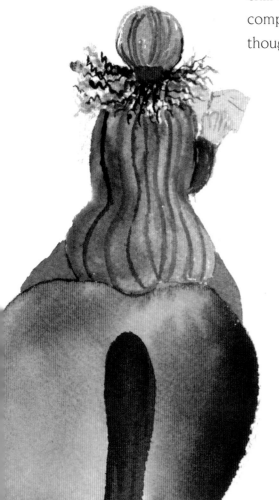

Instead of a delicate scent of roses and lavender, the raw stench of fresh manure cleared our nostrils, and, being fall, the chill of the tack room made it a bit uncomfortable as we completed the required forms. Once the paperwork was done, though, we were ready.

Or, at least, THEY were ready.

Three horses were presented. One for the bride, one for the groom and, you guessed it, one for the marriage commissioner.

I hadn't been on a horse for over twenty-five years!

It's true what they say about riding a bicycle. You never forget. The same holds true for riding a horse. It took a little more effort to get my leg into the stirrup than it may have a few years earlier, but I managed to hoist myself up and, truthfully, it felt like I had never been away from a saddle.

We rode slowly out to a nearby field where the guests were waiting, also on horseback. Fortunately, the mare they had chosen for me was as old as I was and she stood very still the whole time, although the ceremony was punctuated occasionally by snorts and stomps of approval (from the horses, not the guests).

After a couple of shaky attempts, the couple discovered that kissing while on horseback isn't nearly as easy as it looks in the movies, but we nonetheless managed to complete their dream wedding.

And, by the way, the kissing technique?

It just takes a little side-slip of the bride's saddle — and the right motivation.

Perfect Production

"All the guests were mesmerized by the tableau"

Once in a while, a wedding is so original, and planned so perfectly that it truly could be part of a feature film. Some brides are so creative in completing their vision that it truly amazes! From start to finish, this one particular western-themed wedding, was an example of a "perfect production."

THE INVITATIONS: Fabric. All fifty hand-stitched and embroidered by the bride.

THE SETTING: Grandparents' farm. A rustic, highly polished log house. Snowy lace curtains framing each window. One hundred white chairs set up in the side yard. Calico bows tied along the aisles. The lawns and flowers tidied and magnificent with summer blooms. Delicate strains of music floated in the clear country air from "heavens only knows where." The moment was so perfect, it may as well have been fairies.

THE PROCESSION: Two shiny black antique carriages pulled by carefully groomed horses appeared on the horizon and gracefully made their way towards the house. In the first carriage were the bridesmaids dressed in whimsical calico dresses. In the second, the bride, a vision in white, with her proud father.

OUR HERO: Suddenly, from a patch of trees in the distance, two sleek black stallions galloped into sight. They carried the best man and groomsman. Then the groom appeared wearing a nineteenth century formal riding suit, astride a magnificent white stallion. The groom and his men caught up with the carriages and escorted the bride to the gate.

AUDIENCE REACTION: All the guests were mesmerized and I confess I was standing there with my mouth open, staring in awe as the wedding party proceeded towards me. The whole scene was such an enchanting tableau, it took me a few moments to regain my composure and perform the wedding ceremony.

Romance On The Net

"Seniors in a computerized connection"

It is commonplace now to hear stories about cyber-dating and how relationships are forged over the internet. Usually those involved are from the Gen-X crowd. But it isn't always the case.

One particular couple were not only the first "internet"couple I married, but they were also one of my "Golden-Agers." The groom was a retired physician in his late seventies: the bride a lovely American woman in her late sixties.

This was in the very early 90's so they were really on the "cutting edge" of the cyber connections. They met on-line, then spoke by telephone, and after discovering how many interests they shared, they met in person. After dating for a year and getting approval from their grown children, they married. (I'm not sure when our children become our parents but it seems it happens in every family!)

At publication, this mature "computer couple" has been happily wed for over twelve years. So far they are still my only seniors who have connected electronically, but, with computer classes popping up in all the retirement lodges, I'm sure they won't be the last!

Light Up The Sky

"The illuminating presentation will be remembered forever"

A friend of mine is the long-time director of the annual stage show at the world famous Calgary Exhibition and Stampede, the "Greatest Outdoor Show on Earth." After the final performance, he always throws a huge late night party for friends and for entertainers who participate in the extravaganza. One year, there were big surprises for not only the guests and for the director, but also for a good part of the population of the city!

As people gathered in the garden of one of Calgary's heritage homes and were noisily celebrating another successful year, the host unveiled his coup d'état — the party was also his wedding!

Just after midnight, everyone gathered around the couple and I performed the marriage ceremony. The bride and groom congratulated each other on being able to organize the wedding in secrecy but they were totally unaware that they weren't the only ones who could keep a secret.

While celebratory speeches were made, the few friends who were privy to the couple's plans stole away and gave the go-ahead to the other covert operation of the evening — an amazing wedding gift.

At the pre-arranged moment, I invited the bride and groom to look to the southern sky. There, for the only time in the long history of the Calgary Stampede, a second round of fireworks filled the night. Residents of the city, who are long accustomed to the nightly 10:00 display, must have wondered what was going on when the sky was filled again just a few hours later with another spectacular show of rockets, flares and brilliant formations.

No doubt this illuminating presentation will be remembered with joy and awe forever! It was such a fitting "over the top" gift for such a show business groom!

Never Judge A Book By Its Cover

"Appearances are often deceiving"

Part of the responsibility of a marriage commissioner is to provide a suitable place for the ceremony if the couple hasn't arranged a venue. Occasionally I use my home and confirm all the arrangements by telephone, never seeing anyone until the actual event.

As I awaited my intended couple one afternoon, I heard the loud roar of motors — many motors — and rushed to my window. I was slightly aghast to see my driveway filling with bikers.

Rough looking guys. Tough-looking biker-chicks.

I feared a convergence of "Hells Angels," a rumble, a police raid. All sorts of images from television and old movies raced through my mind as I peered around my curtains. I wished my husband were home. I wished our house wasn't so isolated.

Just as I prayed that my picture wouldn't be in the next day's headlines — or obituaries — a wildly-painted van pulled up to deliver more of the exotically-attired, much-tattoo'd wedding guests. Much to my further dismay, there was a huge purple haze hovering over the entire group. My heart raced as I imagined drug deals being done in my tidy little middle class garden.

How incredibly stupid could I be!

The bride and groom were just another couple of kids — very much in love, and very much just "doing their own thing." Their friends were great, too, and, after they left, I noted that they had all been more respectful of my position and my home than most of the "regular" people of their age group I had married. That day I truly learned that you can't judge a book by its cover — no matter how colorful.

The Hockey Connection

"Between periods of a hockey tournament"

Anyone who has a young child in a hockey league understands the early hours and dedication to the sport that make up a season. When the kids are lacing up or cleaning up, the waiting hours are filled with long conversations, so it was no wonder that these two learned of the common values they shared. Over stale coffee, smelly equipment and hectic schedules, they fell in love.

When hockey season ended, and the real dating began, their kids discovered that they could all have a great time together even off the ice. And so it was decided that there was enough substance, love and commitment to join the families within a marriage. And what a wedding they planned!

The next winter, between periods of a hockey tournament, a red carpet was rolled out onto the ice. The groom's team, hockey jerseys over shirts and ties, skated out and formed a straight line as the backdrop for the ceremony while friends and family joined the hundreds of fans in the arena. The strains of the wedding march replaced the usual organ music and caught the attention of customers in the upstairs lounge who pressed against the viewing windows for a better look.

The bride and groom, followed by their children and witnesses, walked down the carpet to Centre Ice where I waited to perform the ceremony.

After the vows were spoken and the rings exchanged, I pronounced them husband and wife and the arena went wild with cheers. At that point, the young hockey players formed an honor guard with crossed sticks and the newlyweds walked off to their new life and blended families.

The reception? Upstairs in the restaurant lounge.

The "head table," of course, was the same table where they had met.

Delightful!

Now Playing At The Palace

"The no-butter policy made sense"

Calgary has a quaint old movie theatre called "The Palace." It holds a sense of nostalgia for some, and an aura of "funkiness" for others. The Palace is more than a theatre. It's a centre of the community and a favorite meeting place. And it was the scene of the couple's first date.

Five years after their first movie together at The Palace, the marquee of the old theatre was ablaze with flashing lights.

"Now Playing — The WEDDING" — with the names of the bride and groom featured as the stars. Passersby were confused — especially since the aging old theatre had been closed the year before but guests were charmed.

The sound and aroma of popping corn filled the air and each guest received a bag of the treat along with a note stating that no oil or butter was available. Before I had time to wonder if this was a touch of frugality, an announcer asked everyone to please take a seat and I was whisked away to the front stage to perform the ceremony.

After the "I do's" were exchanged, the happy couple began their walk down the carpeted aisle and THEN the "no butter" policy made sense. The popcorn was not for eating. It was to replace the traditional confetti and buckets of it were showered over the bride and groom amid cheers of congratulations.

What a sentimental way to get married — in the same place you found love! Truly another picture perfect event.

The Last "I Do"

"The love in the room was overwhelming"

Most people consider "death-bed" weddings only as scenes from movies. Sadly, to others, they are very real and I have had my share of officiating at these very moving ceremonies.

My first such wedding taught me a lot about putting the feelings of others ahead of my own.

Both partners were middle-aged and previously divorced. Together many years, they raised a family, felt married and saw no reason to change the status quo. But no one could have foreseen the onslaught of his cancer. And, unfortunately, pension and inheritance issues can be quickly convoluted or, at the very least, delayed with the absence of marriage documents. In spite of precious little time left to share, this couple knew that it was time to "make it legal."

They cared enough for each other and for their families to find the strength to tidy up one last detail.

I'm embarrassed to admit that, as I approached the hospital, my thoughts were very self-centered. I worried that my emotions would run rampant. I worried that I'd cry. I wondered if I'd be able to perform a satisfactory ceremony under the circumstances. Slipping quietly into the hospital room, I mentally admonished myself: "Nomi, this is not about you. They need your services. Now go do your job!"

I needn't have worried. The love in the room was overwhelming. The nurses who acted as witnesses helped speed up the paperwork and I performed the shortest ceremony allowed and spoke with true empathy.

Murray passed away the next afternoon knowing that he was able to handle the final transaction of their life together. I suspect he is still smiling down on his beloved wife today.

Moonlight & Mushers

"A dream of a winter-wonderland wedding"

The couple from Michigan had come to the magnificent Rocky Mountains with a dream of a snowy fairy tale wedding in the "wild Canadian north." Granted, this was sunny, southern Alberta, and not such a wild place, but it WAS winter and they had a dream and the Snowy Owl Dog Sled Touring Company was there to fulfill it!

One late afternoon, our adventurous group was met by a Snowy Owl van and delivered to their embarkation area where another vehicle was unloading a large pack of Husky sled dogs. The children of the bride-to-be were reveling in this bold new adventure, cheering loudly for each dog unloaded and excitedly following the "mushers" like adoring fans.

The rambunctious dogs were harnessed into their positions at the head of three sleighs. The two kids rode in the lead sleigh with one "musher"; the bridal couple and a musher in the second; another musher and myself at the rear of this comical convoy.

54

Darkness began and the snow sparkled under the full new moon. We made our way through the forest, over a frozen stream and finally to a huge frozen lake. It truly had been a breathtaking ride mushing through the part of the southern mountains known as Kananaskis country! While we waited for a huge bonfire to be lit, we stayed warm and toasty, swaddled deeply in the luxurious furs of the sleds.

Once the flames were high enough to illuminate the entire area and keep everyone comfortable, we clambered out of the furs and began the ceremony. Under the vast navy blue sky, with billions of sparkling stars to add magic, the couple stated their vows.

At the ceremony's conclusion, the adults toasted the couple with icy cold champagne and everyone nibbled on campfire canapés. Luckily, they remembered to bring a camera to record this truly memorable wedding in their private Winter Wonderland!

Better Late Than Never

"Ohmigawd — right day, wrong place"

I have had the good fortune to have very efficient assistants over my career so mistakes have been very rare. But we have had the occasionally "glitch." Case in point: the "late" marriage commissioner — the VERY LATE marriage commissioner.

The "ranch-style" ceremony was to be at the BAR-C — a long drive into the foothills west of Calgary — so we booked it as the last event of the day. With a good friend of mine at the wheel, I headed out with plenty of time to spare.

Arriving at the Bar-C Ranch, however, we saw no cars, no guests, no sign of life except for the odd grazing steer. A ranch hand wandered over and confirmed our worst fears: "Nope. No wedding here today, m'am."

I checked my diary and printed itinerary for the day.
BAR-C Ranch. 4 pm.

Panic set in. (This was before the convenience of cell phones.)

We sped back towards the city and finally found a pay phone at a small town. With my heart in my throat, I dialed my message service and, sure enough, there was a panicked call from the bride and groom. They weren't at the BAR-C, they were at the SARCEE.

OHMIGAWD!!! Right day, wrong ranch!

We quickly called and reassured them that we were on the way. With typical western adaptability, the very gracious family simply served the wedding supper to their fidgeting guests, explaining that the ceremony would be held "with dessert."

Three hours late, the young couple exchanged their vows beside the riverbank in the glow of the setting sun. A happy ending, yes . . . but I don't plan on repeating the same mistake!

Up, Up & Away

"The adventure of being married while airborne"

Hot air balloons float so gracefully across the sky that we sometimes forget they are man-made. Unless you've been involved in the launching of one, you may not know the teamwork and effort it takes. Trucks, tanks of gas, "baskets," balloons — excitement and energy everywhere!

I was as thrilled at the prospect of my first ride in a balloon as my bride and groom were at the adventure of being married in one.

Climbing into the large wicker basket, I looked around for my bearings. Before I could really comprehend the workings of the aircraft, my ears were blasted by a loud "ROAARRR" and we were headed up! (For those uninitiated readers, the large balloon is kept aloft by hot air. This is created by a flame igniting gas in a very loud burst: a long roaring burp every 50 seconds.)

So now you get the picture. One bride, one groom, a witness, a pilot — and a marriage commissioner trying to get through a ceremony a few phrases at a time.

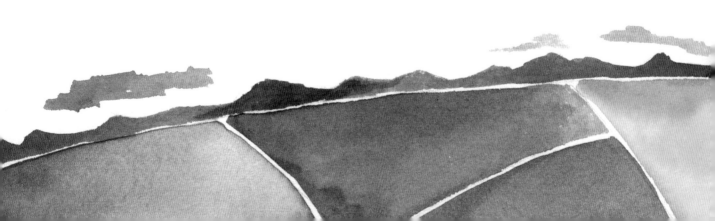

"Dearly beloved, we are gathered here together" . . . "
ROAAAARRRRR . . .
"To join this man and this woman in Holy
Matrimony" . . . ROAAARRRR . . .

Eventually, I got a rhythm going and we
managed to complete the required dialogue.
Ceremony completed, we were all able to enjoy the
breathtaking flight, in spite of the constant "gas
burps." The landing was a different matter.

The basket hit the ground firmly, tipped onto its side
and we had seconds to clumsily disembark. With
rubbery legs, we enjoyed a brief champagne toast
before returning to the reception spot.

This was a delightful experience but, due to the noise
of the gas burps, I would highly recommend a couple
be married on the ground and then celebrate with
their journey into space!

Love Is In The Air

"The majestic Rocky Mountains below"

There is a dining room by the Calgary Airport called "The Flying Club" which is a popular spot for weddings as well as receptions. When I arrived for this particular ceremony, however, I was surprised to be directed outside to the tarmac. And I was further surprised to learn that the bride and groom appeared to be just as confused as I was.

The explanation was right there in front of us — a gleaming new eight-seater private jet, the latest acquisition of the groom's employer. He had decided to give the couple a "Wedding in the Clouds" as his gift.

While the pilot got the engines in motion, I got the paper work done. Then the bride, groom, their respective children, the jet's owner, his wife and myself were hustled aboard.

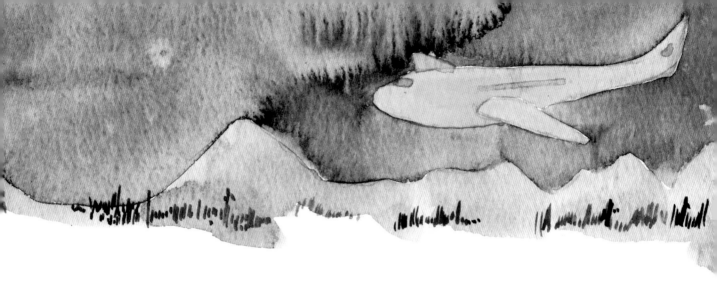

Although I was trying to act as if this were an everyday occurrence, inside I was a bundle of nerves due to the fact that I have a wee tendency towards airsickness. It took intense concentration on the view of both the majestic Rocky Mountains below and the happy participants in front of me to keep my tummy calm. Having a pilot experienced with skirting the bumpy Chinook winds certainly helped, too.

When we landed, an excited group of family and friends greeted the highflying couple with champagne and a wonderful reception

Another unique experience to confirm my love of this job!

You Are My Sunshine

"The resort lived up to its name"

There is a ski resort nestled in the Canadian Rockies called "Sunshine Village." As an avid skier (with limitcd ability) I was excited at the prospect of performing a wedding ceremony at Sunshine and then enjoying a day on the slopes.

The bride and groom were waiting at the first staging area halfway up the mountain. As I disembarked from the gondola lift, I couldn't help but gasp at their appearance. They looked like the cover of a ski magazine. Him, in a sleek black jumpsuit that looked lacquered on; her, in a clinging white jumpsuit, a circlet of white fur around her golden curls, sky-blue ski poles topped with white lilies. Both of them had physiques that Spandex was designed for.

Friends and family joined us and we all took the chair lifts to a second staging area — the beginning of the couple's favorite "run."

The only thing that wasn't perfect was the weather. Clouds had socked in the mountain but we proceeded with everyone in high spirits. After a wonderful ski to the bottom, we regrouped and they shared their oaths of commitment and love.

Then, at the very moment when I encouraged them to share their first married kiss, a wonderful thing happened.

The resort lived up to its name and reputation.

The clouds parted and a golden glow burst through, bathing the mountain in snow-reflected sunshine — perhaps a sign that nature herself was giving approval!

It was a breathtaking moment for all of us.

She Is Of The Devil

"Hazards of the workplace"

Not all of my recollections are of the joyful sort. Some are downright nerve wracking!

I was in the kitchen of the wedding couple, going over final details of the ceremony with the bride and her sister, when an obviously upset older woman appeared at the doorway. She stood staring at me with a somewhat crazed look. Her focus shifted to my lapel pin — the theatrical masks of comedy and tragedy which, unless you're a theatre buff, could appear to be a bit satanic in appearance. Suddenly she pointed to the pin and screamed:

"She is of the Devil. She is of the Devil."

The woman's screams became louder as she became more agitated and the bride gently but firmly guided the old woman out of the room to another part of the house. When she returned, she explained that her dear mother, a devout Catholic, was already upset at her daughter being married in a civil ceremony. And, as she was also in a serious state of dementia, seeing the "devilish-looking" masks pinned onto the jacket of the female marriage commissioner was just too much for her weakened mind to comprehend.

74

After regaining my composure, I began speaking but, as my back was to the bedroom where the distraught woman had been taken, I was more than a bit uneasy and must confess that I rushed through the ceremony.

The poor old soul may have been harmless but after such a sudden outburst, I was having visions of a knife appearing from nowhere and a headline the next day screaming "Marriage Commissioner Victim of Demented Protestor"

As a postscript, I must add that the bride and groom sent flowers, chocolates and wine along with a heartfelt apology and their thanks that I had remained long enough to perform the ceremony. And, I, of course, now fully understood the term "hazards in the workplace."

The Forever Ring

"He carefully held her finger, still tender"

The Dragon Ecstasy. Could this be right? A tattoo parlor?

I was double-checking the address when the door to the exotically painted shop opened and the groom welcomed me.

Both he and his intended were tattoo artists and they wanted to be married in the place where they spent most of their time together. Instead of the long sleeves of a tuxedo, colorful dragons, snakes, hearts and various symbols completely covered his arms. His parents seemed just as bemused as I was at the very original wedding plans but they obviously loved their son and his fiancée and supported their decision. Soon I found myself overlooking the skin art of the young man and just enjoyed his personality.

When we were almost ready, I was called into the back room to meet the bride who was having last minute adjustments made to her hair.

I was surprised to see that her only visible tattoo was a dainty group of daisies on one arm. She was a pretty young girl and sweetly asked if I'd like to see her wedding band.

I thought it was unusual that she already had her ring, but then, as she raised her delicate hand, I realized why it could not be given to her during the ceremony. There, on the traditional "second finger, left hand" was the groom's gift. An exquisite tattoo circling her finger — his symbol to her that his love would be as forever as his wedding band.

During the ceremony, at the point where rings are exchanged, he carefully held her finger, still tender from the tattooing procedure, and gently spoke his vows.

They were a lovely couple and in spite of the unusual location and unique choice of ring, they showed such sincerity and commitment that I left feeling they would be one of the couples who really had a good chance of "making it".

Housewarming To Heartwarming

"You could have heard a pin drop — even on new grass"

One special couple had been living together for a great number of years, and the renovations to their home had been going on for just as long! In fact, the project was taking so long that friends and family invested time, energy and even cold hard cash to ensure that it was finally completed and once it was, a major party was in order! Even the local Mayor was invited to "cut the ribbon" to officially open the rejuvenated home.

With the guests filling the front yard, and the owners each holding one end of a wide ribbon in front of their new front door, the Mayor dramatically sliced through the satin band. The new front door opened to reveal — ME, in my official "marryin' robes."

To the great surprise of everyone (many of whom believed these two would never get around to tying the knot) the bride and groom stood side by side and spoke their vows. Keeping non-traditional, they gave each other uniquely-designed, original bracelets.

You could have heard a pin drop — even on newly cut grass!

Once the ceremony was complete, the party erupted in hoots of delight — and maybe a bit of disbelief.

The housewarming turned into a heartwarming!

After more than a dozen years, I am pleased to count this couple among my close personal friends.

Drop-In Groom

"There was no sign of the groom"

Pigeon Mountain is a failed ski resort in the beautiful Kananaskis Country of the Alberta foothills. Left behind from the financial fallout is a charming and rustic lodge that is available for many types of gatherings — including weddings. It's quite a long drive from the city so many groups use charter buses, or, at the very least, drive in an organized "convoy" to ensure the safe and timely arrival of everyone.

The time for this ceremony came and I was there, ready to fulfill my duties.

The beautiful bride and her attendants were ready. The families and guests were ready. But there was no sign of the groom and his best man.

As minutes ticked by, the bride became concerned, no doubt wondering if her young man had changed his mind at the last minute, or had been in an accident, or . . . ??? She nervously giggled to me that the groom's absence certainly hadn't been in HER plans.

Suddenly, there was a loud whirring noise that quickly became very intense, the sound amplified by the deep valley walls. Closer and closer. Louder and louder. Then, right above us, two helicopters appeared, hovered for a moment for dramatic effect, and landed right beside the parking area.

The groom and his buddies had arrived. And in such style!

Once the laughter subsided, the ceremony was completed and then all the guests were treated to helicopter rides over the magnificent Spray Lakes area and Kananaskis Valley.

It was a spectacular event in every sense of the word!

Coffee, Tea Or Wedding?

"The bouquet was luncheon broccoli"

My husband and I were returning from a conference in California, enjoying each other's company on the long flight home.

After we had been airborne for about an hour, we heard an announcement from the Captain.

"Is anyone on this plane licensed to perform marriages?"

The young couple had planned to marry and honeymoon in Canada. Once their flight had begun, however, they had a romantic notion that an airplane pilot, like some sea captains in the past, were also licensed to perform wedding ceremonies and they thought it would be "cool" to be married in the clouds. Fortunately, when the Captain was unable to do their bidding, Nomi was there to save the day!

All the passengers were invited to become part of the big event and all, save for one cranky fellow who preferred to nap, got right into the celebratory spirit. My husband became the official photographer, a flight attendant escorted the bride, others volunteered as "maid of honor" or witnesses and the galley crew made a little bouquet out of salad broccoli.

Over applause for the bride and groom, the Captain and crew gave the newlyweds a bottle of champagne — their first wedding gift.

And, just as my husband and I were
chuckling at the gift wrap (an airplane
barf bag closed with a Delta Airlines
pin), the crew presented us with a
similar one in honor of the wedding
anniversary we were celebrating. The
wedding had taken place north of the
49th parallel so my Canadian license
made things legal and the next day,
the couple purchased their marriage
license and completed the paperwork.
A little backwards, but . . .

Later, when I wrote to the CEO
of Delta Airlines complimenting
his charming and accommodating
personnel, he responded with
amusement and gratitude!

Almost Disaster

"It wasn't a pretty picture!"

A typical wedding in a big hotel. The bride getting ready in one room, the groom and his attendants in another. I popped into the bride's room first.

Utter chaos! The small room overcrowded. The bride's gown was too big. Bridesmaids and flower girls were flitting about passing bouquets and applying makeup. Cameras flashed every few seconds.

In the midst of this mayhem, the door opened and the bride's uncle (who was to be giving her away) "floated" in on a wave of alcohol fumes. Not only was he totally plastered; he was loudly lecturing his niece on how to preserve a marriage, peppering his diatribe with crude four letter words which added to the bride's dismay. I snuck out while she tried vainly to protect the youngsters from his profanity. Tapping on the door of the groom, I was hoping for a change of pace. No such luck. His pallor was not a good sign. "We forgot the rings."

While his best man reassured him that someone had been sent to retrieve them, two little boys ran past in their underwear. "Oh, yeah. We forgot their tuxedos, too."

What else could go wrong?!

94

I returned to the bride's room for a status check. It wasn't a pretty picture.

"Uncle John" had passed out cold — not on the floor, but directly on the bride's train AND a wee flower girl. Happily, the child wasn't hurt and we managed to get the old fool onto a bed. Another uncle was summoned to give away the bride and everyone calmed down in Room Number One.

Room Number Two was also coming together. The boys were dressed, the best man had the rings and the groom was ready to say, "I do." The wedding party and family finally gathered in the hall and I took my place in front of the hundreds of guests, ready to begin the ceremony. I cleared my throat and began to speak. Nothing. Silence. No microphone. Fortunately, I have a big voice and for that ceremony I darn near bellowed.

"Murphy's Law" (whatever can go wrong, will go wrong) was truly tested that day, but we all got through it with flying colors!

Beadwork In The Badlands

"A big thank you to the Great Spirit"

When I am advised that sink holes, hidden mine shafts, biting insects, cacti and rattlesnakes could be possible uninvited guests, my hair stands up on the back of my neck and I lose my enthusiasm! But, I had committed to performing this particular ceremony so I was not going to back out.

In Drumheller, Alberta, the famous Badlands are very similar in terrain as the U.S. Badlands in North Dakota, a place Sioux Indians called "Mako Sika" (land bad). In Canada, early French trappers called them "les mauvais terres." My wedding venue was a spectacular viewpoint called Horseshoe Canyon. Dinosaurs walked there seventy-odd million years ago! The canyon is filled with stunning coulees and formations called "hoodoos" (sandstone columns) created by centuries of erosion.

The wind in the Badlands has a ghost-like presence and shadows from all the formations take on shapes that fire up the most vivid imaginations.

The groom was a very spiritual Ojibwa Indian and he had traveled all the way from Toronto to be married in this almost-sacred place.

He arrived wearing a magnificent white deerskin shirt, covered in the most beautiful intricate beadwork I had ever seen.

The bride wore a white deerskin dress covered in the same elegant beadwork. The effort had to have taken months and months of loving and painstaking attention to each detail of the authentic native design.

The surprising aspect was that the bride, a non-native, had made the garments herself. With no prior experience, she had created these extraordinary masterpieces as a sign of respect for her groom's heritage.

Their personalized ceremony combined the standard marriage vows with traditional native customs including the burning of sweet grass. I felt very privileged to have been a participant in the union of these two wonderful people.

And, oh yes, I also said a big Thank You to the Great Spirit for keeping the rattlesnakes away!

A Very Pregnant Wedding

"I had TWO people to be concerned about"

It was another summer wedding and the day was becoming very "close" and sticky. The front room was elegant and appropriately set up, but it was very small and I began to have a bit of concern for the bride. She was VERY pregnant and I wondered if she would be comfortable in the heat with all the added pressure of the wedding.

When the rest of the bridal party entered the room, I immediately discovered that I had TWO people to be concerned about. Not only was the bride pregnant, so was her maid of honor. Late in the third trimester, she was looking paler than her light summery dress. I kept watching both the young women very closely as I began.

Sure enough, half way through, the maid of honor keeled over face first.

Needless to say, everything came to a quick halt. Cool heads prevailed; damp towels revived her and, assured that no harm was done and with heart racing, I continued the ceremony. The celebration and reception, though somewhat subdued, carried on as planned without further incidents.

Years later, I had the opportunity to meet both of the women again. Both babies had thrived and become lovely, healthy children. Although it had been a scary few moments at the time, the "very pregnant" wedding had become a focus of laughter at many family gatherings.

Forever Young

"For the heart — it's never too late"

When the caller asked if we gave a "Seniors discount," I was so amused by this original enquiry, I told my assistant to say YES and give them a special rate.

The wedding was set for a charming community center called "The Red Barn."

The groom was a tall, handsome man. He was attired in tasteful Western garb and, although he certainly looked like a "senior," I was shocked to see he was ninety years old. (I would never have guessed he was a day over 75)

And the bride? Well, she was just a "kid" in her seventies.

They laughed as they described how they met.

"We were on our way to Emerald Lake on a Seniors outing," the groom said. "We didn't know each other at all. She was seated a couple of rows ahead of me and got up to get something. The bus jerked and she fell backwards. Landed right in my lap."

He paused to stretch his arms high and wide for emphasis.

"And THAT WAS THAT."

His bride laughed and echoed:

"Yup. THAT WAS THAT!"

These two amazing, energetic people just filled me with joy. Their love was so obvious as they hugged and kissed all through our conversation. And their wedding was also full of joy, witnessed and celebrated not only by friends but also children, grandchildren and great-grandchildren!

They were a true example of how love knows no age. And, for the heart, it's never too late!

And that's that.
Just some of my favorite weddings.
 I hope you've enjoyed being a guest.
There are so many more stories to tell
but we can leave them for the next time.

Love,
Nomi